VINEGAR BONE

This book was supported by a grant from
the Greenwall Fund of
The Academy of American Poets.

WESLEYAN POETRY

VINEGAR BONE

MARTHA ZWEIG

Wesleyan University Press
Published by University Press of New England
Hanover and London

Wesleyan University Press
Published by University Press of New England,
Hanover, NH 03755
© 1999 by Martha Zweig
All rights reserved
Printed in the United States of America   5 4 3 2 1
CIP data appear at the end of the book

Intaglios by Elinor Randall

CONTENTS

III. A TOKEN DUST

ACKNOWLEDGMENTS

Poems in this collection, some in slightly different form, have appeared elsewhere as follows: *Anon*, "Density"; *The Beloit Poetry Journal*, "Message"; *Bitterroot*, "A Witch"; *Boston Review*, "Bad Fish" and "The Fleet" (reprint); *The Carleton Miscellany*, "No Child"; *Catalyst*, "What You Hear From Home"; *Chicago Review*, "Mother, Daughter" and "Others"; *Chiron Review*, "For Peter"; *CPU Review*, "Morning"; *Ellipsis*, "Precedent"; *Epoch*, "The Bargain" and "The Hill"; *The Falcon*, "Healing"; *Fine Madness*, "Blue Light" and "Waking or Not"; *Generation*, "Demonstration," "The Pain," and "Solipsist Behaviorism"; *Green Mountains Review*, "Dictum" and "Moon, Mother, Clown"; *Invisible City*, "Death of the Air," "From Among The Missing," and "The Undead"; *The Journal*, "Oblivion" and "Three Days"; *The Kenyon Review*, "Sick Day"; *The Little Magazine*, "Questioning the Sex Killer"; *Mānoa*, "Death Escort"; *The Massachusetts Review*, "Fidelity"; *The Minnesota Review*, "Lycanthropy"; *New Letters*, "Immaterial"; *Northwest Review*, "Divination," "Spooked," and "Spring Sentiment"; *One Art*, "Taking Her On" and "Moon, Mother, Clown" (reprint); *The Sow's Ear*, "For Resurrection" and "The Mermaid Wife"; *Sumac*, "Vinegar Bone"; *Zone 3*, "Burying the Cat."

"Two" was first printed in *National Forum · The Phi Kappa Phi Journal*, Vol. 75, No. 2. "The Fleet" is reprinted from *Shenandoah: The Washington and Lee University Review*, with the permission of the Editor. The poems "Space Raptures" and "Transfer of Energy" originally appeared in *The University Review*, Vol. 33, No. 3 and Vol. 34, No. 2. They are reprinted here with permission of *New Letters* (formerly *The University Review*) and the Curators of the University of Missouri–Kansas City.

The Vermont Council On The Arts published the author's chapbook, *Powers*, which included: "Dark Song," "The Hill," "Live Alone," "Morning," "No Child," "Others," "Questioning the Sex Killer," and "Steep." *Mānoa* reprinted from *Powers* a selection including: "Dark Song," "Live Alone," "No Child," and "Steep."

Naomi Shihab Nye and Paul B. Janeczko included "Dark Song" in their anthology *I Feel a Little Jumpy Around You*, New York: Simon & Schuster Books for Young Readers, 1996.

I thank:

the University of Michigan, which gave Avery Hopwood and Jule Hopwood Awards to manuscripts which included: "Demonstration," "Density," "The Pain," "Solipsist Behaviorism," "Space Raptures," and "Transfer Of Energy";

CPU Review, which reprinted "Morning" as the winner of third prize in its 1993 poetry contest;

Georgette Perry, of Catamount Press, who included "Others" in *Witnessing Earth*, an anthology;

Heather McHugh and Reginald Gibbons.

July 1998   M.Z.

I. PRETTY TRICKERY

BURYING THE CAT

Now the cat won't keep coming back
like this loose snow
that hurls past and then drops down
into the four dirt corners where all touches stop.
Curled fall leaves still scrape
and skid over from the yard next door.
It's a blowy night out, and clear;
gusts clash.
The multicolored other
cats interweave and yowl.

All night,
without resort to torture, the winter
moon's oldest
methods elicit from the
ground this brimming ghost light.

Pats with the back of the shovel leveled off the top.
They ache
from the cold under there
where they are held,

and once again there are more
dead things than ever before.

PRECEDENT

When Death was a baby—this was before
either here or there had vicinity or
coming or going had yonder, before
any light, before dark, when time had to tell
itself & ignorantly, neither tock
nor wax nor tick nor wane—then Death blinked so

amazed to exist that it thought there must
have been a mistake bigger than Daddy,
& thrummed in its coop; almost it could guess,
by the bazillions, animal, vegetable,
mineral souls staggering in dominion
before it, whinnying, blistered, aghast.

Death was too tiny then to seize even
the first least one, before there even was one.
It swam into its zeal, in the steep urgent
swells of exaltation choked & paddled;
took a great notion—*They'll never hear the end
of me now*—but it grew up to be Death.

BAD FISH

Hours on end unobserved in its
humming tank, the bigger fish
of two has killed the smaller, has eaten it up
nearly half, from the tail in. Bad big fish,
you'll patrol your lurid
cubicle all alone now!

In its heyday, the dead one, speedy
damsel who shimmered slinkiest purple & green,
a bad fish too, repeatedly ambushed &
terrorized to death the third,
white-banded red one, tomato clown,
not a bad fish, I regret it.

Last fish, you big one, lengthy turquoise
& green luna wrasse, roll your eyes,
eat your heart out, binge, loop over & binge glass
wall to glass corner,
you can see me, fan the slits
of your bright particular gills

at my nostrils & sneer for now,
then watt off queenly, swirl
into coral labyrinths all to yourself: might-as-well
be endless Möbius wiggle-room
you conform to & monopolize, you mouth, you
anus, you beauty.

HERE

From chilly space, how could
a star do human people any good?
They followed because it seemed to them that it led:
it stopped them at their own flesh and blood
on sour straw in the animal shed.

QUESTIONING THE SEX KILLER

He did it deliberately &
so when the police tracked him down he was
able to explain it so
clearly they had to
agree. Still, they hadn't *done* it.

Anyway, he'd checked it out &
it was what they'd suspected,
women! —women just
opened & spilled, there was
nothing so special in there after all

FLOURISH

O bicker later! early
August preoccupied
reloading berries for bear
diverts us unnecessarily, yet why
not? veer up among posh waist-
high ferns, clump by blunder.

Round and gifted hill! —it
shoulders our every visit, it
bluffs us, shies off lights,
tosses shades in the birch tops
after birds; instantly the birds
ruffle back and switch twigs.

High spirits, assist us! a pretty
trickery crimps the loose path,
ravels us with heat & green
lilts in a thicket of squanders,
spotty prodigals, tufts underfoot of
pink arbitraries & vertigo.

A WITCH

She likes it down in the well.
In the circle of day or night light
at the bottom of the motionless air
at the top of the motionless water, she
fluctuates in rings.
All anyone knows is she
must have followed a stone somebody
tossed down there, or else she was one.

THE HILL

Everywhere the mouths
of their holes occur,
saying, *There are other worlds.*
Let the topologist step through.
And, *Kiss us, kiss us.*

When a man kisses a woman
or two men or two women
kiss, an animal may run through,
storing the grain in two places
for the mother of the litter

of their next life
and her tiny blind ones.
The hill keeps the woodchuck, the mouse also,
and the striped garter snake, at its dark
entrances to say so.

DICTUM

This morning I find written on my
stones the laws of happiness.
No runes, plain English.
Truly my meadow, but I'll
tell you too. That's one.

No fool, you know already
just how these teasers run.
They take themselves back,
& leave you exactly as before
but in a shimmering vacuity,

so you won't mind that the next
one says, read your own stones,
& that the third—there are always three—
says, just before it
does, *we vanish.*

THE FLEET

When space puts to earth
Something of what it is
The wet ground stows it,
Or the sugary leaves do;
As the moon winnows the fish, all
Of them breed in its huge haul

A stock of changes;
Rays pepper and criss-cross
Creature from creature
From race from kind to the end
Of all of their permutations.
Suppose that the ships are real:

They scout where they go
For anyplace neutral.
Everything alive
In their husbandry attends
Each landing to find it is part
Of the same expedition.

SOLIPSIST BEHAVIORISM

Our skins, though we know
only them of each other,
intrigue ingeniously. Though you are not
nearly so real as I am, I
am easily taken in,

absorbed by your
unsubtlety, your sex, your making up
of instant nonsense songs, your hairiness
and skill at skipping stones,
all wholly wonderful

When I have a fit
of fright about dying, it concerns
my own self exclusively, and yet you
charm me as the stars do, that the dark
should have such objects in it:

I should prefer to die
fortunately, under stars, clear-headed;
or if, as is probable, stars
are not available, I should be well served
that you stand in my sight and perform, twinkling.

FOR PETER

You call out you're here and I call come in:
you come in my summer, you
come in my sun and my green,
you come in my happy body and my sleepy dream.

I live alone; if the wind
ruffles my pretty acres I'm proud,
I'm an open stone, plain through,
and live in the meadow.

You're a charm,
somebody dark I wanted,
big grin star to star and
wicked like the toad whose

love is so sweet and odd
that she wants him slippery and
cool to the clasp as he is,
knobby, no prince.

NEWPORT

I could still smell his wrist.
He greased my blood;
I wanted his bones.
In days we would be common knowledge.

June sun polished Newport.
Where we dropped our feet lake Memphremagog pushed its
swells clear over from Canada & slapped under the rickety marina;
it might muffle the lust,
maybe we'd get air.
But we'd wriggle to go at each other anywhere.

We suffered!
We hadn't mated nearly enough.
I drove us home. Blue cloud
shadows sped the little car through such sunny
spaced blows I thought we'd buckle,
& then I'd take the green ditch
grass licks in my pelvis, almost anything would do.

THE MERMAID WIFE

Early this morning I flicked out after your upstart
dreams again, neighborly male
human head. All speckly &
parabled they looped about our bed
& at walls glanced upwards: I shooshoo
them to see what they'll do, & just to keep them going.

It used to unnerve me, is why I didn't say
when I first knew, that neither nor both
of us ever will go now.
Long since, though, I've turned quite as shameless
in constancy as in all else, & my day after day
again dawns freshly disreputable.

Let me explicate doom, dear love:
the irritant exotic
sexual imagination's failure at last,
as if long ago that summery opaque blue
seascape horizon had, unbeknownst &
exactly then, engaged its two bright

rims all around to seal us in:
enchanted, I'm sure, largesse of tideline
pickings & lifewreck. I'll smooth us another
bosomy high dune so we can watch
the ships farfetch—they go quickening by
as if the pretty ocean might lick itself dry.

VINEGAR BONE

In a school science demonstration, a bone
soaked in vinegar softens overnight.

No child's affection grasps
The gist of the vinegar bone,
Nearness of the amoeba,
A Christian horror.
Run a finger down the
Spine of a second grader,
Mark the central assertion
To which the plasm adapts:

The boys grow tall, chest-proud,
And the girls' limbs turn shapely
Who twisted the vinegar bone.
But a gradual night sourness
On the cell walls of their own
Sense calls up the ruinous
Fluid and its smell to be
Thrust in the face of God

Who touched the man in his bone
As he dreamed, turned the rib supple,
Caused it to bow into beauty;
Made the woman who ever after
Must twit the man's body,
Provoke and sap his rigor:
Proof, when the two grapple,
Of the sleep they slump into as one.

II. NEAR THING

WAKING OR NOT

Just beyond our air blows the black sky.
Each morning, here, when the streaked turtles nudge
each one another in the gold mud, they are waking
all of their part, and part of our part that we
may or may not wake.

So they struggle against our sleep,
urging the world that has living turtles in it
and the lake, its mud edge,
and the sun that hatches their eggs,
not dream turtles, or a dream lake, or any dream eggs.

They are struggling to raise the real morning.
We can feel the shove and jostle of their shells.
Up from under the shells if they die
will come blowing snatches of the black sky
instead of turtles' breath, for dreams, that they deepen.

MESSAGE

When is no harm done?
Mother called. What did she want?
—the joy noise, put into words.

But I was long gone, I was out herding the dead
East to their other pasture
& I nodded off in their bells. The water

steered us so far abroad in its avenue
—it was so willing & so mild—
that we took to bewildering among ourselves;

we could hear faint praise
for our lives dispersing grass to grass,
so we knelt there, leaning our heads

low among the buttercup bees while it lasted,
bee visits dusting the pistils
of our ears,

until, shifting their several barely
tenable voids, my charges
gathered up on their slight bones again

& admitted the airs that then plucked
them off to vanish. They went with the last
of my name & the names I knew in their mouths.

Maybe sometime will I wade the cool
humdrum morning prattle from the springs
down to where it first widens & stills

& lightly touch a finger upon the clear
pool shallow there—zero, a vowel, ten, twenty
unanswerable rings?

MOON, MOTHER, CLOWN

Moon sour berry,
moon sour berry,
weren't you the white clown of the sky,
didn't we travel in the cloud bottom, and
didn't all the dogs holler together
hi hi:

Moon bitter bone,
bitter old moonbone now,
you rose then like a clown mother head,
I rose then like your little one: I'd
be little moon, I said, ever ever
after you won't I?

This big around it
was, a moon this
big around grew, it was you, you
said hop follow and spangled me, so I
grew, look I still prance the ruffly lake in your paint, true face,
your bright girl:

Why why thin ki-yi dogs,
why why thin
moon pinch, moon hump and cripple? Oh race
me out to the three rings, tummy lady,
squat waddle and pull me out of your body
lock-and-tumble:

triple moon around do a double
moon-and-a-half,
cock and watch
me toss and juggle my babies head-over-heels all the black-and-
glitter night long. Tip us the seven oceans,
every blessed bright salt drop.

SPACE RAPTURES

First of all, they train the raptures out
So well that some maintain there never was
Anything to fear of them, as though
That was all a dreaming; and, in fact,
The man who stepped outside kept to his golden tether.

Still, who would not
Get an inkling, of the world hung
There, likely to be missed, and stars not up
But on all sides flung out
Under and over, and on through the dark, and we
Too in our various
Craft gliding along theoretically?—

Just as, on earth, we reach and pass
Between flesh and other
Shining objects, never quite grasping.

IMMATERIAL

I have laid the heat of my womanly
love low. Why is that?
It is less than a furrow.

Faithfully the scruple of love instructed me,
& tipped the weight & measure
I gave my word
to honor an unusually
lingual man, or a child, but now what only
remains to catch at, & to speak of,
sparks surefire & derives where else? over

there, where the woollybear caterpillar goes,
rippling its bristles.
Menial thing, takes it forever.

What trinket surprises me,
recognizably mattering?
                              Mumbling
beggars with cups, welcome to you: each
gets this one-half
pinch of the ashes my mother
is, until they're all gone.

STEEP

It must have been the sloppy
boots: he tripped on some
bent root the leaves hid and
went down. When whatever his
hands grabbed gave, he
remembered about being born: it
was cold suddenly,
someone helped.

If he moved at all twigs
snapped in his sleeves. He
felt acorn caps prick the
wrists inside his
damp gloves where the blood
vessels under the watchstrap buckle
pushed and pulled. Leaves
brown and green cooled him.

He remembered about being born:
he slid out slack and gooey.
There was nothing
there but the cold
air he had to
let inside him, had to drag in;
someone helped,
hands held him.

HEALING

It can happen anywhere.
A cut simply closes. The edges
join like two spills.

Cramped up in hiding
the felon watches his gut wound
out of his keenest eyes.
How did it get in?
               All the ransacked
rooms never shocked any
householder more. But it heals

like drawers that pull themselves back
in, fold and straighten their layers out
smooth and seed the wet new
jewelry in between:
strings, clusters, studded clasps.

So the rich man
will handle the skin of the rich wife again.

NO CHILD

You can't get children with a parrot feather,
can't get children by a trick knot;
can't get children in a wheel, in a moon,
on a rib, in a root, in a slit;

No blood, no hair starts you children,
not in your any pit or crotch;
no pocket, no button, no braid,
no trim or snip of you or stitch;

Firefly light's so cold,
clean sheets so white,
under you over you night and night
rain flood and rain rinse,

Snow drift and snow gust
sill and eave, post and rut, your
heat never rubs you sweats you any child,
crease fold wrap cotton and linen;

Save the mice ribbon, the owl wool,
litter and hatch, hatch and litter,
give jays the thread and leave
the rat out a bright cord;

Gold circle silver clasp,
then sun up in the morning moon down,
skinny arm next to a skinny leg in
bed bitten a little bitten

Can't get a child for a year and a year,
can't get a child whether now whether then
in fright and trouble, thin dry sticks a
cold child doesn't strike in, doesn't catch.

MORNING

You hollering dreams!
Finish up with Sierra now,
get done with Sierra;
pick up all her things,
put all her things back in her tall cupboard.

Dreams better get yourselves out of her scrapes in a hurry:

unfasten each other and take off her terrors,
unzip their shiny backs,
pull them off you rightside out
and hang them up, all her empty monsters on her hooks;

haul down her banners,
fold her landscapes,
collect her cities,
put all the caps back on her powers.

The mommy face goes where it belongs,
the daddy face goes where it belongs,
the house goes in the snow,
the horse goes in the livingroom, it's

going to be bright, it's
going to be breakfast.

Dreams you always do leave her a messy wild head of hair.

THREE DAYS

1.

Today rain
runs this outfit, I
can't start a thought or operate
six buttons & a spoon.
Bad break; stands to lose.
I'll put the rain
to work then, make it make my
bed, cook up my buttery
lunch egg & do the dish.

2.

Dustkitties mind
my business back behind
that orange corner chair.
They bat the dumb luck scraps around, such
hairs, threads & stubs of prayer
as daily drop.

3.

Slept too long, I woke wiry;
thought a red mare
bucked under the thunder, she
hollowed & banked, the gate
clipped her pretty flank, I
got myself dressed,
hurried out there,
she billowed & stared.

SPRING SENTIMENT

Mud time always sucks back his steps, he tells her.
He's the pickpocket victim, the marked man.
Stars take after his poor threads, & in bed
death itself in his soft yellow teeth snacks.

She in her littlest kiss soon gives him the slip.
She wants to watch lively if the snow slumps low yet,
if the ice slacks awry; she wants to shake out light
snappy like best linen when it's time & wants it time.

Pity attend their spirits, & yours & mine,
pity to stir up a warm mist in the dooryard,
pity alone to work the odd weeks ahead or they'll
doom, they'll null souls. Near thing: it depends.

PERCUSSIVE

Tin husband—the cookie-cutter, disgrace
of my middle years—struck up the kettle of mineral
deposits over the blue flame & clashed
toast & jam. It's because of long-suffering
breakfast six of his letters didn't timely
stuff & evacuate what rural-route box?—
minutes ahead of the next-best delivery
dogs' postal jaws. Scuffle: that'll be the dogs now.

Remember love? No. I think of a spring-driven
bicycle bell's tremolo but that's childhood, nobody
riding but me into my birthday. Horsechestnuts
dropped & cracked, the husks popped off. Sunlight, some
from inside the eyeball, fluttered the screen between
what was me & wasn't: never know what to make
of your own body, which even your poor face is, chipmunk
cheeks! —Auntie Alarming tweak them & I screech.

Just one irritable word, clap hands & banish me!
I'd go live in a pony's ear, that swivels: subtle hairs
tickle to pick up parade drums faint from downtown
where this one never marched yet, the pony I mean,
with the ears. Dull thuds of distant children, civic officials
& their auxiliaries—but High Street switches aside at me
listening, tips every last soul of them up & off that
precipice where the rocky surf booms, & now dead-ends.

TWO

Often they both could swear
they overhear their
deaths converse. But which is which?
And they never can make out the exact words.

Months seem to go by.
They hang new yellow cups on the
cupboard hooks. The dreaming
dog scrapes in the upstairs hall and they

know what that noise is. But
then the deaths resume their talk, talk,
just aside, benignly, one or the
other voice almost exactly like the other.

Whenever she thinks that now she will
leave him she must always also
imagine her death leaving his death,
how one will turn out

to be hers, it will get up
loosely and excuse itself from the other
one, which will be his. He
knows this is why she stays.

THE PAIN

Suddenly waking to dark from a dream
instantly forgotten,
I find my belly
traversed by a small
pain, back and forth, inside.
It has come upon me in my sleep.

It seems no indication, but
fully established, and
living there like some
snail in a stump,
going about its business:

in this featureless room, this compliant
silence, and I not having kept watch,
it has come and got all
time until morning
allotted to its industry.

SPOOKED

Chipper enough though he kept
in her nastiest scraps, he's dumbed
since in the lull long rid of her,
& apprehends his heart's cramps as the
bobcats just aglow

who, he always knew, huddled singly upon each
dusk in the maple crooks over
her old dirt road,
              & who tonight
formally drift their
critters' lazy yellowish eyes
from there to him here in his keen disarray;
who narrow him down in his own
street: pitchdark & he's prey.
                        Or so momentarily
under a breath & in one jaunt step he puts it:

Dearest claws I may ever
have true hope to go under, scant
not my poor shrugged shoulder & caved loin,
but hold fast there, & wherever, & tug me out
in gobbles to your satisfaction, I'm such
easy gore, I must've missed the
love something terrible this time.

BLUE LIGHT

Those are the stars,
who knows what they are like?
They are not like us.
This is my kiss goodnight:

Goodnight, the stars
do not have any kiss out there;
in here where we are, you are
the one I kiss, little blue light.

Stars are more than human people.
Stars are almost all there is;
you were born little and smart and lucky
to turn up in the stars and dark,

and so was I born lucky
to a mother lucky-born,
child and all and child and all,
born one, born another.

Once I kiss you goodnight and go,
try yourself what the stars are;
try how near, how far they are,
try what their distance is for:

kiss goodnight, the stars will change
past window and window again and again;
if we change, change us back again,
blue light and me, goodnight,
blue light and me, goodnight.

WHAT YOU HEAR FROM HOME

Someone could get there to meet you, if not
we ourselves, then a friend or neighbor, some
town official, or he could send a car,
there'll be a number you can call to call
a car, & just in case you feel you need

a place, we've so much room we never use.
Other than that, little to tell. We saw
some men, youngish, with big fingery hands
—this was on TV—out of the school you
went to they made stones. Three had invented fire.

Last afternoon we got to talking on
you & your brothers, for some two hours, things
you don't know, things you'd never remember,
but we do, all by ourselves. It's strange, it
makes you wonder whose lives they must have been.

We need less. Each day's list comes up shorter.
We get new maps if anything changes.
Hourly we have excellent reports of
weather. We're happy, & for the first time
in our lives we do not expect to die.

CURSE OF THE BABIES

Lightfooted daddies on
splendid adventures,
we are your growing sperms
who dropped off their tails.
Now we suck thumbs &
knead the blankets.

Our eyes occasionally
hit on focus. We
thump in cribs but we
come from outer space, it was
black, it was far away, it
stung stars. Now we wallow

chubby & dimpled, we
curry favor like the underdog,
we pump our new knees,
we slobber & grab &
coo coo & thrive from
our tummies & gain.

You were who? But we were
nobodies. Someone delivered us.
Someone named us. We recall
nonentity, the fleshless bloodless
singleminded shameless dark,
& thither we recommend you.

DEATH OF THE AIR

Are we short spells in our heads, or what?
Tired out chasing, selves bed down.
Wind lays snow in skeins around,
Tugs and overlaps, nest-building.
All night the covered shells mend.

It's bare as a moon out,
Deep in dust, ice-dry.
The air's gone. The last drifts lie
Just as the thin air left them,
Year after year on all.

Sleep, households and neighborhoods.
Then dream light struck on the crystal matrix;
The eventual few going by who
Compact the splinters the snow's
Fallen in. Dream their tracks.

Dream courtships, in moonskins.

DEMONSTRATION

See, just so: one can pinch
Gently the cat's paw exactly as
One pinches a snapdragon

For exactly the same intriguing
Spreading and opening, and curious
Yield to the fingers;

So that the toe's sheath gives out
Smoothly its clear claw (not yet
Fierce, for the cat believes you are playing):

Whereupon the claw itself imagines
Fangs for the snapdragon,
Otherwise why such a congruence in
The great plan of things?

Each being necessary, the cat goes
Forever on paws which are flowers,
And, in the garden, the innocent summer
Dragons become literal.

DENSITY

Just now, out of rigid silence,
Miles away, a freight went by:
Put ripples into the dark.

Its whistle sounded so
Faint it was barely trainlike;
Still it seems
I could ride those waves,
Gently, as a boat does,
Bobbing on crest and trough:

Except that the very thought's made
Of the fact that my head wrecked it,
There in the way, cutting the whistle off.

HOW I KNOW

Mother carried Julie home from fireworks,
Julie sang asleep my mommy's strong,
and the whole moon
stayed through all the fireworks,
we were up late,
I remember, I

thought the moon's face got all
blurry because it was dead,
big dead face coming out in the sky in
July, it would blow its kiss first to
Julie then me,
would it hurt us a lot? But

mother said how the fireworks worked,
how they shot up so high and why
four colors blew one out of another: she
said people made them to do that and
people were setting them off so
everybody could see. So I

could see too, and Julie could And no
big dead moon kiss caught
any of us, then or ever. There isn't
any such thing. This is
how I know. Julie and I slept all
night like baby sisters.

THE UNDEAD

One is not
oneself exactly.

The personal corpse
sealed in the dark
dreads rupture,
cannot turn anywhere,

is occupied, finds
there is this other, a
not certainly human
movement begun within it

the grave
baby & growing

FIDELITY

Little indeed to say about the sex part.
Could be I wrote something
similar in a letter I don't
remember very well.
                        Seaside: I was on rocks.
Noisy salt water
smacked over fizz. It pushed the thick brown kelp up,
dropped it limp, ran off, rose;
simplicity itself.
                  Truly a day's
windy sunlight fades out once to pearl.
Back then clean sand
skims my belly even now, this same
belly I left behind
there, dear as I knew it was to be after &
covered with male kisses.
                     Not
long now & the stars pick out black dark.

The best of love turns out
lifelong & not human. This
floozy brilliance.

PETIT-BOURGEOIS

The murderers' gift is to sort facts as
reasons to kill you or wait.
They have to figure out which.
Sleep rolls us among their hunches,
dream and next dream,

while our main chance
is that nothing much out of
the ordinary ever happens,
usually they wait,
many of us live a long time.

Meanwhile & with luck in their work the
murderers hit on ways to
run through possibilities over
again faster & faster: it's
then you hear the

sun hum the
wind sing in papers the
power crackle & see
faces flash & the
money really glow

OBLIVION

Landfill dozers churn over offal &
there in it three sturdy plastic
palominos persist forever, whose
child never missed them at all

once his father whistled him in, so
late it was, after one of a great
many days all jumbled together
& during which he forgot much else:

three more of his first beagle's
nicknames; where he hid the letter
he wrote to himself; how to catch a dropped
stitch, how to knit at all, another camp song

& the route of Magellan, whose sailors
gnawed oxhide fittings & lipped
at the last of thick yellow water
while the passage heaved.

MOTHER, DAUGHTER

She got out of me
a new body, and nicer;
when her fists open up
her hands show luckier lines
and she is no woman.

She's got my death in her life,
cross, gossiping oaks,
but that is not what I hate:
she'll die, you trees will, we can
wring stones' throats too, if we want. It's that

now she's growing, she doubles and triples herself
while in me my eggs only
gather my blood
and pinch out one by one
to be somebody else or nothing.

SICK DAY

Mama, I came down
pup-sick among the bureaucrats!
Inside my skin I felt fever choose
me the way shame regularly
used to, on the playground.

Home,
rumple-bedded, I keep stumbling mostly
by accident upon myself in & out of
lurid sleep hourly. I called &
called for you but you were dead.

But I cried! & it didn't do any good.
It would if you cared,
like the other mothers.

ANIMA

For some reason utter dark
opens. Once born, always
starry then, even in the iron hand.

TRANSFER OF ENERGY

Sometimes in fall I got my chance
At the heaps of leaves:
I dived spread-eagled,
Thrashed and scuffled the pin oak and maple
And sneezed at their smells.
I was all cells and veins.

Then the yard man, taking over,
Bullied me with the rake and flushed me.
I jumped in the play of my skin, not nearly
Spent, but the leaves held a shadowy
Form in the tense
Space I leaped out of:

It was dusk, and still. I crouched there, amazed,
As the shape my body left of its movements blazed.

LYCANTHROPY

Household objects had faded and slipped their uses.
From handling them I was turned otherwise
to the early moon in the doorframe.

A gap had opened in time
and in habits of life and mind.
Between the ranged houses the moon was emerging

(as all of our shapes flagged in the dropping sun
whoever looked): it laid loosely a sheen on
that scarcely showed. When I came out

a little, as far as the stoop,
spots of the moon were still of a blended blue
in the sun's sky, unembodied.

It was neither day nor night.
For a half hour nothing was dominant.
The meanwhile made us possible. Then as

dark and the bulk of the moon clarified, I
too came to light, and being thereby
fleshed, edged out into the victory gathering.

THE BARGAIN

Look, the birds' acute angle, their
intent clip south in the glossy weather:
so high nothing distracts them
as we are distracted, watching;
and they are not free.

This too is propriety,
that the prick to a change of country
will not prompt all
in the same way or degree,
and many, though they tremble, stay,

in their fixed animal part.
But this was another life
jingled by on its way like the traveling carnival man.

Leave of my senses,
axle, spokes, wheelrim;
a token dust settles with the matchmaker.

FROM AMONG THE MISSING

Whose are these limbs
that lead from the leaves in?
Her both hands hold in the tree.
The leaves cloud around like minds
her wrists. Does this ever happen,

that there lift to the wound nests
strands of senseless hair, then the
thin twigs enter the veins,
before the next heartbeat the
sap reddens, the trunk and branch bark split

like snakes through to her new skin?
Then all thought changes.
Yet it was innocent, fathers;
in a look of the noon green,
in desire from among the missing,

your oiled girls sunbathing
got up filled with light
and tended towards the woods leaving
behind them these bright towels
on the grass, and their singing radios.

OTHERS

In the roots of
dark so tall it goes out past the sky
we rock the sleepy children in
their zipped jackets,
in their own smoky hair smell.

Stars advance along the maple branches

and the next lives approach among the
children's ribs,
glint through the growing bones.

This story tells of the
animals who draw near
the fire circle
while a story of animals who
draw near the fire circle is told.

Their eyes their
strangest part lead our
orange light back into their brains.

LIVE ALONE

I sleep
next to nothing,
next to nothing
sleeps my
dumpy body sleeps my mussy head;

lettuce head,
cabbage head,
sleep green, sleep grown,
no hurry,
sunny breezy bed, clean brown furrow;

cat watch a
crow, cat
catch air,
catch shadow,
yawn stretch me my dream's tail-end:

live alone,
get old alone;
who'll know,
who'll say
boo to get a pennysworth of
anybody's little life back?

TAKING HER ON

She starts a false fire, it
catches my meadow dry &
baffled in birds, she
hurls false water down my rocks
into limpid false pools.

Nobody trifles her business,
she does wild schism &
diametric, she kens &
savvies me senseless. I
will speak to her:

listen, I say, I'm here, I
showed up, you're mad,
I know you'd as soon
stiff the stars as entertain
my heart your meat, but

you will come to terms.
We will settle concerning
this maple. That it puts
one red stem out to
each leaf. Doesn't it.

DIVINATION

Where this forked stick
yanks down hard you'll
find what your throat
wants now,
pure water,
and for when that's
gone the stone you sucked
it from to die against
years later.
Grip the two arms,
walk as if the
footprint opened in the
ground ahead for your next step.

DARK SONG

Don't be scared of the dark:
in your tidy room in the dark there is
no hard heart;
you slip into your bed in the dark
like a secret into an ear,
dark to repeat it, dark to overhear.

Don't be scared of the dark:
all night is is the biggest shadow,
little kid in the biggest shadow, it's
how you can tell the sun's behind the world
when the sun's gone,
when the sun's gone.

Day gone, daylight gone;
think about dark to all the things with no-eyes:
how dark cools off the meadow stones,
how dark stops the sugar work in the leaves,
how dark bends the tall grass
stalks over all wet. Don't scare

easy of any
such deep deep dark, how it is, the
toys, your favorites, turtle, cat,
stuffed and buttoned; and who
carries you keeps you, dark doesn't, no dark
doesn't, I do.

DEATH ESCORT

Look out how things
look at night, mother let
me find our street &
soon soon we
see stars crowd the block,

how to get home, which
house here has which door, it's
easy, mother I
dream I guide you you
step in little shoes from

each step I show you
to the next,
younger, younger;
only the
trees make it seem

strange
when they crisp their
leaves like
ladies & address us
late pleasantries,

mother this time let me,
see, here, put
your hand, you
know the latch,
let me open the dark.

FOR RESURRECTION

Dear bones,
bare bones of me dead,
I want you to joint
the rain puddle together & hoist it
up so that the water walks;
make of my beggarly
stalk & shuck
again an intricate high carriage.

University Press of New England
publishes books under its own imprint and is the publisher for Brandeis
University Press, Dartmouth College, Middlebury College Press, Univer-
sity of New Hampshire, Tufts University, and Wesleyan University Press.

ABOUT THE AUTHOR

Martha Zweig is the author of *Powers* (a chapbook with Vermont Cross-
roads Press, 1976). Her poetry has appeared in journals, including *Beloit
Poetry Journal, Chicago Review, Kenyon Reveiw*, and *Massachusetts Review*.
She lives in Hardwick, Vermont.

Library of Congress Cataloging-in-Publication Data

Zweig, Martha

Vinegar bone / Martha Zweig.

p. cm. — (Wesleyan Poetry)

ISBN 0-8195-6358-7 (alk. paper). — ISBN 0-8195-6359-5

(pbk. : alk. paper)

I. Title. II. Series.

PS3576.W37V56 1999

811'.54—dc21 98-47526